FLORENCE NIGHTINGALE

Richard Tames

W

FRANKLIN WATTS

LONDON•SYDNEY

Contents

This edition 2003

Franklin Watts
96 Leonard Street
London
EC2A 4XD

Franklin Watts Australia
45-51 Huntley Street
Alexandria, NSW 2015

© Franklin Watts 1989, 2003

Series Editor: Penny Horton
Designer: Ross George

A CIP catalogue record for this book is
available from the British Library.

ISBN 0 7496 5019 2

Printed in Belgium

A Reluctant Lady of Leisure

Apart from Queen Victoria herself, Florence Nightingale became perhaps the most famous woman of the Victorian age. She won her fame by challenging and changing the attitude of people towards women and what they should do with their lives. But for the first third of her life she tried obediently to live quietly and unadventurously in the way that was expected of a woman born into a wealthy and respectable family.

Florence Nightingale's father, William Edward Nightingale, was the son of a successful Sheffield banker. He inherited country estates and a lead mine in Derbyshire and was rich enough to buy another estate in Hampshire. He was a man who knew how to enjoy his good fortune. He did not need to work, although he served as High Sheriff of Hampshire to fulfil his sense of public duty. His personal interests

Florence Nightingale, brought to fame as "The Lady With The Lamp".

Florence's father, who offered his daughter a privileged education.

Family entertainment in the drawing room of a Victorian household.

were reading and travel. In fact, both his daughters were born in Italy, while he and his wife were enjoying a two year honeymoon. Both children were named after the cities where they were born – first Parthenope (the ancient name for Naples) and then Florence.

The Nightingale family followed a comfortable yearly routine. The summer was spent in Derbyshire and the rest of the year in Hampshire, where Florence's mother, Fanny, had dozens of relatives and friends who were invited to dinners and parties. Twice a year the family made extended visits to London for further rounds of entertaining, shopping and amusement.

Little was required of the Nightingale sisters except that they should make themselves pretty and pleasant to others. "Parthe" enjoyed doing this, but Florence did not. Increasingly, Florence annoyed her mother and delighted her father by choosing to spend her time reading in his large and extensive library, rather than amusing guests in the richly-furnished drawing room.

Above: **Florence, an eager pupil, often read in her father's library.**

Florence acquired an education rarely given to girls at that time. But it was an education strictly for its own sake. Florence's father had no intention of educating her for any purpose, much less for a career. He believed that her education would simply make her a more agreeable companion and, in due course, a more cultured wife and mother.

In 1837, when Florence was 17, the whole family set off on a tour of Europe. Uncharacteristically, Florence pleased her mother with her new-found passion for dancing. She was an attractive young woman and could be high-spirited when she wanted to be. At formal dances in Geneva and Genoa, Pisa and Paris,

Below: **Queen Victoria. Florence was presented to the Queen in 1839.**

Mr Nightingale, because of his leisurely life style, had both the time and the education to become the perfect teacher for the eager and hard-working Florence. A graduate of Cambridge University, he taught her Greek, Latin, French, German and Italian, as well as history and philosophy. Parthe tried at first to follow the strict daily timetable set by the girls' father but fell further and further behind. Finally she stopped attending lessons altogether, preferring to help her mother with household tasks, embroidery or flower arranging, which were thought to be suitable for a young woman of her position.

Between the ages of 12 and 16

Florence was determined to avoid the life of idleness shared by well-born women of the Victorian age.

she was the belle of the ball.

In 1839, following the custom of the day, she was presented to the young Queen Victoria, along with dozens of other well-born women of her age. One long summer was passed in London, dancing and entertaining. Slowly Florence began to realize that her education was over. A life of idleness stretched before her. Nothing would be demanded of her beyond "endless tweedling of nosegays in jugs". Florence had nothing to do and it made her angry. But she loved her family and genuinely wanted to please them. She did not wish to complain or upset them. Even so, she was determined not to waste her life. She could not see the point in studying without purpose and the thought of marriage horrified her – being tied to another person for life and trapped in a world where supervizing servants would be the hardest task demanded of her.

Florence asked her parents' permission to study mathematics because it was difficult and would be a challenge. Permission was refused. Florence accepted graciously and turned instead to the only kind of "work" her parents could not object to – visiting the poor and sick.

Nursing before Nightingale

Florence's admirers have given a grim picture of the typical nurse before Nightingale to emphasise the importance of her reforms. At best they saw the old-style nurse as a maid servant fit for washing linen, lighting fires and cooking. At worst she was shown as drunken, dirty and idle. However, many nurses were caring and learned to ease their patients' suffering. But they were undoubtedly drawn from the servant classes and certainly had no formal knowledge of medicine.

The inspiration for the idea of professional nursing came from the Roman Catholic church, which had developed **orders** of nuns, who in caring for the sick showed their Christian love. Many were well-educated and some even came from the highest ranks of society. Their **habit** was worn like a uniform and they were certainly used to a disciplined way of life. But their commitment to nursing sprang from their religious faith. It was not an end in itself, still less a career.

Florence Nightingale made it possible for women of any class to care for the sick, for a salary they need not be ashamed to take.

Below: **St Bartholomew's Hospital, London, in the 1840s when nursing was seen as an improper profession for a woman of Florence Nightingale's background.**

The Will to Work

Crowded streets were breeding grounds for disease in the 1800s.

England in the 1840s was a country in which there were great contrasts of wealth and poverty. Rich people, like the Nightingales, enjoyed their way of life but also felt they had a duty to help people less fortunate than themselves. Usually this task was performed by the women of the family and consisted of caring for the very old, the weak and the sick. Nursing, in this amateur sense, was seen as both a Christian and a lady-like pastime.

Florence Nightingale began her nursing career, because of this, by visiting the cottages of the poor and ill on her father's estates. She began by taking round small presents of nourishing food, but soon progressed to simple nursing tasks such as making sure the sick were clean and comfortable. She quickly realized that nursing could be a truly satisfying form of work. She also realized that it should be practised with system and method, as well as kindness and care. Nursing could, in

other words, become a "profession". But she had no idea how she could become more professional, though she knew that what she needed was "experience, not patchwork experience, but experience followed up and systematized."

Florence Nightingale began her nursing education by volunteering to look after sick relatives in their own homes. Her parents, proud of their daughter's kindness, readily gave their permission for her to leave their house. They suspected nothing of her desire to escape, so that she could learn and work.

When she was 24, Florence asked her parents if she could go to Salisbury Infirmary, a charity hospital, to study nursing for three months. Her family were shocked. Her mother wept and her father called her "ungrateful". At the time, professional nurses were seen as

little better than servants. Faced with such opposition, Florence at once gave way. It was probably the anger within her that caused Florence's poor health, leaving her nervous and exhausted. Her family decided that she needed a holiday.

In Rome, Florence met an important British official, Sidney Herbert, who was Secretary to the Admiralty. He recognized in her both a fine mind and a strong character. He encouraged her interest in problems of health and poverty. When she returned to England, Herbert introduced her to a wide circle of friends interested in the same issues. They were all respectable and respected people. Her parents could hardly object. Herbert also introduced her to *Blue Books*, the enormous official publications which set out the results of government enquiries into the problems of the day.

Knowing how strongly her parents disliked her interest in medical matters, Florence proceeded to educate herself in private. Getting up before dawn, she would sit in the silence of her own room, devouring hundreds of pages of reports and statistics about drainage problems or outbreaks of disease. Then when the rest of the family got up, she would join them for breakfast and go through the rest of the day playing her part in their social life and domestic duties.

In 1849 a successful young journalist, Richard Monckton Milnes, proposed to Florence. Mrs Nightingale always hoped that marriage would take Florence's mind off nursing once and for all. The family were thrilled. Everyone liked him – including Florence. But she refused his proposal all the same. She later confessed in her diary that " ... since I refused him not one day has passed without my thinking of him ... ".

But she was determined to stick to her decision:-

"I know that I could not bear his life, that to be nailed to a continuation, an exaggeration of my present life without hope of another, would be intolerable to me – that voluntarily to put it out of my power ever to be able to seize the chance of forming myself a true and rich life would seem to me like suicide."

Once again the Nightingales decided that a holiday was required. This time it was to be a cruise to

Above: **Sidney Herbert, who encouraged Florence in her career.**

the Mediterranean. Florence obediently went. But on the way back she fitted in a visit to the Institution of Deaconesses at Kaiserswerth, near Düsseldorf in Germany. The Institution was staffed by single or widowed women, who were inspired by their Protestant religion to follow the example of Roman Catholic nuns and give their lives to the service of others through teaching, nursing and generally caring for those unable to care for themselves. The Kaiserswerth Institution contained not only a hospital, but also two schools, an orphanage and an asylum for the mentally ill. It did not actually give formal training in nursing but it could certainly give volunteers the opportunity to learn by experience.

The Middlesex Hospital where Florence Nightingale volunteered to nurse cholera victims in 1854.

Florence was inspired by Kaiserswerth and, perhaps because it was a religious foundation or perhaps because it was abroad and out of the way of local gossip, her parents finally relented and gave her permission to go back.

Florence returned to Kaiserswerth in July 1851 and worked like a slave for three months. 'I am as happy as the day is long,' she wrote to her parents. And her days were very long, beginning at 5.00 am and continuing well into the night.

Back in England once more, Florence found herself playing nurse in turn to her father, sister and grandmother. Once more, Florence put her duty to her family before her ambitions. But she continued to show her commitment by visiting hospitals as far apart as London, Edinburgh, Dublin and Paris.

Salvation came unexpectedly through the offer of a job as superintendent of the recently-founded "Institution for the Care of Sick Gentlewomen in Distressed Circumstances" in Harley Street, London. Florence accepted the offer eagerly. Her mother and sister were appalled, but this time her father took her side and gave her an allowance of £500 a year. This was enough to make her free of all money worries and able to live her own life as she chose. At 33, Florence Nightingale was finally accepted by her family as an independent adult.

Nature itself gave her promotion into the front line of nursing. In the summer of 1854 cholera broke out in London, and Florence volunteered her services to the nearby Middlesex Hospital as superintendent of the nurses caring for victims of the cholera **epidemic**. It was dangerous and demanding work – an ideal dress rehearsal for the adventure which would make her a national heroine.

The Crimean War

When war broke out between Russia and the Turkish Empire in 1853, Britain joined France, fighting the Russians. The British government's main concern was to prevent the Russians from taking territory from the weak Turkish Empire and building bases which would enable their navy to operate in the Mediterranean. The war was popular in Britain because public opinion was already strongly anti-Russian. The British, proud of their constitution and parliament, saw the rule of the Russian **tsars** as little better than **tyranny.** They were also repelled by the brutality with which the Russians had put down popular national risings in Poland (1830–31) and Hungary(1848–9).

In September 1854, 50,000 British and French troops crossed the Black Sea, landed on the Crimean peninsula and attacked and laid seige to the fortress of Sebastopol. On 25 October the Russians were thrown back when they tried to seize the British base at Balaklava. On 5 November the battle of Inkerman saw the failure of a second attack. The war dragged on until February 1856, when Austria threatened to join the allies. Russia then agreed to demolish its Black Sea forts and withdraw its ships from threatening Turkey.

25 October 1854. British and Russian soldiers clash as the British forces fight to protect their base at Balaklava.

The Lady With The Lamp

The outbreak of war against Russia in March 1854 was greeted with wild enthusiasm in Britain. But by the autumn the public mood had changed dramatically, largely as a result of the **dispatches** of the war correspondent of *The Times*, William Howard Russell. While the wounded soldiers of Britain's ally, France, were carefully nursed by trained and disciplined Catholic nuns, British casualties were dying at the Turkish hospital in Scutari for lack of the simplest nursing services.

Russell's questions thundered out like a criminal accusation:-

"Are there no devoted women among us, able and willing to go forth and to **minister to** the sick and suffering soldiers of the East? … Are none of the daughters of England, at this extreme hour of need, ready for such a work of mercy? Must we fall so far below the French in self-sacrifice and devotedness?"

On 14 October Florence Nightingale wrote to the War Office, offering her services. On the same day her old friend, Sidney Herbert, now Secretary of State for War,

Above: **William Howard Russell, war correspondent for *The Times*.**

Left: **Wounded soldiers of the British Army had no decent facilities for recovery before Florence's nursing mission arrived at Scutari.**

The hospital at Scutari, where the nursing mission set to work.

wrote to her, hours before he received her letter:–

"I receive numbers of offers from ladies to go out but they are ladies who have no conception of what a hospital is, nor of the nature of its duties … My question simply is, Would you listen to the request to go out and supervize the whole thing? You would, of course, have **plenary** authority over all the nurses and I think I could secure you the fullest assistance and co-operation from the medical staff and you would also have an unlimited power of drawing on the government for whatever you think **requisite** for the success of your mission."

Three days later Florence was hastily organizing a nursing team. Florence was assisted by Lady Canning, founder of the Institution for Sick Gentlewomen, who was greatly impressed by the mission leader's powers of organization:–

"She has such nerve and skill and is so gentle and wise and quiet; even now she is in no bustle or hurry, though so much is on her hands, and such numbers of people volunteer their services."

The nursing mission arrived at Scutari on 4 November, the eve of the battle at Inkerman. The barrack hospital was vast, filthy and ridden with disease. A week later one of the nurses described conditions at the hospital in a letter home:–

"There were no vessels for water or utensils of any kind; no soap, towels or clothes … the men lying in their uniforms, stiff with gore and covered with filth to a degree and of a kind no one could write about; their persons covered with vermin … We have not seen a drop of milk and the bread is extremely sour. The butter is most filthy … the meat is more like moist leather than food."

Despite Sidney Herbert's promise that the medical officers would welcome her with open arms, Florence met with suspicion and resistance. Army officers and doctors alike regarded the dispatch of the nursing mission as a criticism of their own efforts in trying circumstances and many of her own team were clearly inexperienced.

Florence realized that, whatever Sidney Herbert's wishes or authority, he was thousands of miles away in London and it was up to her and her nurses to prove their worth by deeds, not words. Nor was nursing, as such, the first of her priorities, as she made clear in a hasty letter home:-

"I am a kind of General Dealer … A whole army having been ordered to abandon its kit … I am now clothing the British Army … I am really cook, housekeeper, scavenger … washerwoman … storekeeper."

Florence Nightingale, at Scutari, nursing sick and wounded soldiers.

A tough, efficient attitude, and the realization that no amount of nursing could help a patient who was not basically clean and well-fed, enabled Florence and her team to take command of the situation. Within days of their arrival the members of the nursing mission found themselves faced with a flood of new casualties, as Florence recorded on 14 November:–

"On Thursday last we had 1,715 sick and wounded in this hospital (among whom 120 cholera patients) and 650 severely wounded … when a message came to me to prepare for 510 wounded … arriving from the dreadful affair of Balaklava … We had but half an hour's notice before they began landing the wounded. Between 1 and 9 o'clock we had the mattresses stuffed, sewn up, laid

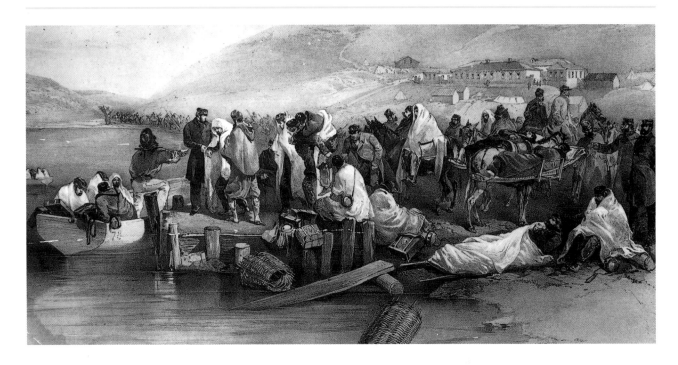

down – alas! only on matting on the floor – the men washed and put to bed and all their wounds dressed … The operations are all performed in the ward … no time to move them."

By the end of the year Scutari hospital was transformed. A kitchen and laundry were established to serve not only the wounded soldiers but also the wives and children which many of the patients brought with them. Food and supplies, paid for by a relief fund, organized by *The Times* newspaper, had begun to arrive. And in December a further 46 nurses arrived.

Above: **Wounded soldiers leave Balaklava by boat for Scutari hospital.**

Left: **One of the many improvements made at Scutari during the war was a kitchen for soldiers and their families.**

Florence Nightingale fought dirt, delay and disbelief. She fought by persistence and persuasion but, above all, by example. It was said that she was on her feet 20 hours out of every 24. It is certain that she forbade any other woman to be in the wards after eight at night, when nursing duties were handed over to male *orderlies*. But she herself continued to make rounds into the early hours. The wounded therefore named her "The Lady With The Lamp" and it was said that they were so devoted to her that they would kiss her shadow when it fell on their pillows.

Although Florence created order out of chaos in a matter of weeks, it took her rather longer to turn a breeding ground for disease into a safe setting for recovery.

The year 1855 opened with an alarming increase in the number of deaths at Scutari from cholera and typhus. The losses included seven army doctors and three of the nurses. Harsh conditions in the frozen trenches around the occupied city of Sebastopol led to many further casualties suffering from

Florence spent the majority of her time at Scutari with her patients.

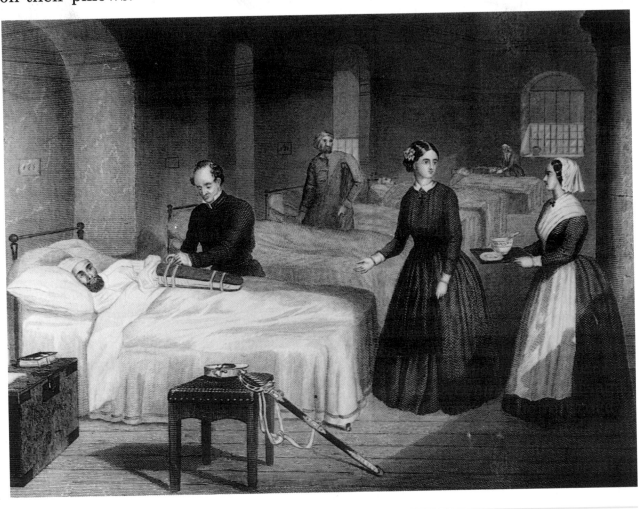

frost bite and dysentery. By February, four out of ten casualties entering Scutari died there.

Florence Nightingale knew that the problem was a simple lack of decent sanitation; not enough efficient drains, no working lavatories or clean water. The answer was "sanitary reform". Once again the persistence of "The Lady in Chief" paid off when the War Office finally listened to her pleas and ordered the necessary work to be done. By June, the Scutari death rate was down to two per cent and Florence felt free to tour hospitals near the battlefield at Balaklava. The expedition nearly cost her her life when she contracted a

Severe weather conditions on the battlefields of Sebastapol led to a sharp increase in hospital patients.

dangerous infection and lay for 12 days on the edge of death. But as soon as she recovered she went back to work in Scutari.

The war ended in March 1856 and Florence returned to Balaklava to supervize the evacuation of the wounded. She finally left for home in August, with the last casualties. Declining free passage on a British warship, she returned privately on a French vessel and went back to her family home in Derbyshire. Meanwhile a grateful nation waited to adore her.

Sidney Herbert

Wealthy, intelligent and handsome, Sidney Herbert was also a devout Christian who gave away much of his fortune to charity. He visited Florence Nightingale while she was nursing and encouraged her interest in hospitals. As well as working at the War Office, he was to serve as honorary secretary of the fund to establish a nursing school in Florence Nightingale's honour and as chairman of the **Royal Commission** on the health of the army. He worked so hard at this task, travelling round, inspecting hospitals and drafting reports, that he destroyed his own health.

Florence was not aware of just how ill he had become. She thought she was dying herself and desperately needed him to push through her reforms. Pressed by her, he took on the additional task of chairing the Royal Commission on the health of the army in India and of reforming the War Office itself. The strain was too much and he died in 1861. Florence was stricken with grief and declared, "I know of no widow more desolate than I". She always marked the anniversary of his death with a day of prayer and meditation.

Dr John Sutherland and Robert Rawlinson, members of the sanitary commission, set up with the help of Sidney Herbert.

The Reformer

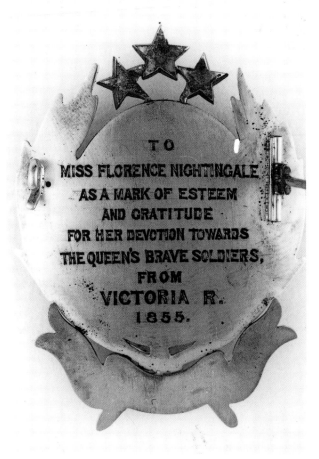

The front (left) **and back** (right) **of the brooch presented to Florence Nightingale by Queen Victoria.**

National admiration for Florence Nightingale was led by Queen Victoria herself. In January 1856 she wrote a personal letter of thanks, accompanied by a brooch designed by her husband, the Prince Consort. This unique gift combined symbols of religion, beauty and **patriotism** – a red cross, for her efforts abroad; a royal crown of crystal in a bed of lilies, for purity; and, encircling them, a blue band, with the words "Blessed are the merciful".

In September 1856 Florence visited the Queen at her Scottish summer residence, Balmoral. She came, not to bask in royal praise, but to seize the chance to press at the highest level for action on behalf of her next cause – the reform of the army's whole medical service. After her visit the Prince Consort noted:–

"She put before us all that affects our present military hospital system and the reforms that are needed: we are much pleased with her. She is extremely modest."

Florence was determined that the British Army should never again find itself in the same chaos as it had created in the Crimea. Only effective reform could in some way save the lives of thousands of soldiers needlessly lost through incompetence. She had no doubt that severe problems remained in peacetime as well. After inspecting hospital facilities at Chatham she declared that they were:–

"Another symptom of the system which in the Crimea put to death 16,000 men. You might as well take 1,100 men every year out into Salisbury Plain and shoot them."

Although she was now a semi-invalid, exhausted by her efforts, Florence wrote a constant stream of letters to government officials and influential politicians, pressing for the appointment of a Royal Commission on the health of the British Army.

Queen Victoria's first visit to wounded soldiers at Chatham, 1854.

A Royal Commission was eventually appointed and Florence herself submitted a long and confidential report on the workings of the army medical service in the Crimea, based on her own experience, for its consideration. Reforms did at last follow as a result of its recommendations. In 1859 an army medical college was opened at Chatham in Kent. In 1861 the first military hospital was established at Woolwich in South East London, and in 1862 a permanent army sanitary commission was appointed to ensure that these new practices for the British Army were enforced and kept up to standard.

During the Crimean War Florence organized the establishment of a laundry at Balaklava hospital.

Florence Nightingale's work for army medical reform raised her status still further, from national heroine to international expert. During the American Civil War (1861–5) both sides tried to apply the lessons she had learned so painfully in the Crimea. When the war ended, the Secretary of the United States Christian Union wrote to her to say:–

"Your influence and our indebtedness to you can never be known."

Meanwhile Florence's interests had taken on another international dimension – the health problems of the British Empire in India. In 1857, when a great rebellion broke out among troops of the Indian Army, she wrote to her old friend Lady Canning, whose husband was now Governor-General of India, offering, in spite of her own poor health:–

"to come out at 24 hours notice, if there was anything for her to do in her line of business."

She never went to India, but the health of both the army and the people of that vast subcontinent became one of her lasting interests.

The British government appointed

The rebellion of the Indian Army in 1857.

a Royal Commission on the sanitary state of the army in India and when its report appeared in 1863 a copy was sent to Florence Nightingale for her comments. They came back under the typically brisk heading, "How people may live and not die in India". Her remarks were separately printed as a pamphlet and sold by the thousand.

But if her thoughts were often directed at problems far away, there was one other cause to which the restless reformer was equally devoted – the reform of nursing education itself.

The British in India

British contact with India began through trade, but the gradual collapse of the power of the ruling Mughal emperors, led to a general British takeover by the middle of the nineteenth century.

The main aim of British rule in India was to maintain law and order, stop bandits, settle disputes and collect the taxes needed to pay for the army, police and other officials.

The British presence also led to the building of railways and efforts by missionaries to spread the Christian religion. Such changes seemed to some Indians an attack on their traditional way of life. The outcome was a great rebellion in 1857. Most of the army, however, stayed loyal and British rule was re-established by force.

British officials tried to improve the welfare of ordinary Indians by organizing the building of roads and the digging of canals to drain swamps and irrigate dry land. They also set up hospitals and schools. But the sheer size of India made the task of improvement immense. A harvest failure or an epidemic could leave the authorities faced with a disaster quite beyond their powers. In 1877–8, for example, a single famine killed no less than four million people. The task of tackling India's poverty and disease needed all the Florence Nightingales it could attract.

Life was often hard for Indians under British rule. While the British led a luxurious lifestyle, many Indians still suffered terrible poverty.

Nightingale Nurses

Even before Florence Nightingale had returned from the Crimea, a public meeting in London had decided to raise a fund to establish a training school for nurses, named in her honour and following her methods. It was the only public honour she agreed to accept, though for the first few years she had little to do with it. She considered army sanitary reform to be a more urgent task. Nevertheless she appointed a council of nine men to take charge of the public money collected and supervize the creation of an "Institution for the Training, Sustenance and Protection of Nurses and Hospital Attendants". To guide its discussions Florence wrote a short book which became her most famous published work – *Notes on Nursing: What it is and What it is not.*

The Nightingale School of Nursing was established in 1860 in St Thomas's Hospital, London. Its first superintendent was Mrs Wardroper, who was also Matron of St Thomas's and had Miss Nightingale's personal confidence and approval. The highest standards were demanded of **probationer nurses** from the start and only 15 were accepted for the first, one year training programme, which was organized by Mrs Wardroper, rather than by Florence herself. The probationers, dressed in plain brown uniforms, lived together in a wing of the hospital. All their expenses and living costs were paid for out of the fund and a pocket money allowance of £10 a year was also provided.

The actual training given to probationer nurses was, for the most part, practical, and included such skills as bed-making, the application of **leeches** and the dressing of wounds. It had been Florence's firm intention that training should also include lectures on anatomy and other aspects of medical knowledge. But nobody was clear just what the lectures should actually cover and it

Nightingale nurses pay tribute at a statue of Florence Nightingale.

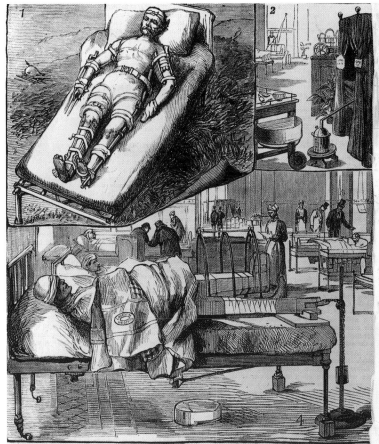

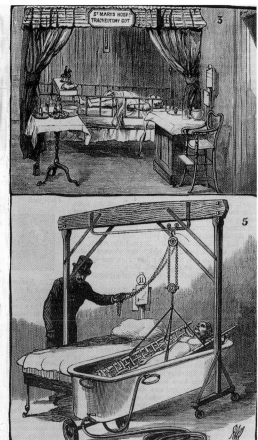

was quite obvious that most of the probationers were too poorly-educated to be able to learn much from them anyway. So the details of the training programme evolved through trial and error, becoming more demanding only as the new profession began to attract women with better educations, coming from wealthier families.

Florence was herself called upon to exercise self-denial as her own parents' health began to fail. Cut off from public life she devoted herself to nursing her father through his last illness between 1873–4 and then caring for her mother until her death in 1880.

At 60 Florence finally found herself free of family obligations. But she also found that many of her oldest friends had now died. She realized that it would be easy for her to become first of all isolated, then lonely and finally embittered. With her usual practical wisdom she decided to work hard at being agreeable and useful to those around her, often ending her many letters with the bidding, "Should there be anything in which I can be the least use, here I am." Tormented by idleness in her youth, exhausted by her work in her middle years, Florence Nightingale dedicated

Dec 16/96
10, SOUTH STREET,
PARK LANE, W.

Dear Duke of Westminster

Good speed to your noble effort in favour of District Nurses for town & country; and in commemoration of our Queen who cares for all. We look upon the District Nurse, if she is what she should be, & if we give her the training she should have, as the Great civilizer of the poor. training as well as nursing them out of ill health into good health (Health Missioners), out of drink into self control but all without preaching, without patronizing — as friends in sympathy. But let them hold the standard high as Nurses Pray be sure I will try to help all I can, tho' that be small, here I will with your leave let you know. Pray believe me your Grace's faithful Servant

Florence Nightingale

Left: One of Florence's many letters written in her later life offering assistance to friends and colleagues.

Below: The house where Florence Nightingale enjoyed her later years.

herself to enjoying her old age, surrounded by flowers, visitors and young relatives with their babies. She was an excellent cook and a charming hostess and her home was not only beautifully kept, but light and pretty as well.

For the first time in her life, Florence Nightingale felt free of the pressure of having to choose between work and people. Her ambition to serve a great cause had made her appear hard, unloving, even ruthless. But her life had been full of quiet acts of personal kindness. When she returned from the Crimea, for example, she brought with her a personal following of waifs and strays, including a one-legged sailor boy, a badly-scarred Russian and a puppy, presented to her by the troops. All these she looked after at her own expense, without fuss or need for praise. And no Nightingale nurse ever went to a new post in a strange part of the country without finding flowers there to welcome her. This softer side of her nature was often obscured by the stern style she used in her professional life.

Florence Nightingale's last years were quiet. After 1896, she never left her London house again. In 1901 she became almost blind, a great blow which finally halted her lifetime passion for writing letters. In 1907 King Edward VII awarded her the **Order of Merit**, the first time the honour had been given to a woman. In 1908 she was given the **Freedom of the City of London**. But these tributes meant little to her. For the last six months of her life she also lost the ability to speak.

Florence Nightingale died in 1910. In accordance with her wishes there was no great public funeral or burial in Westminster Abbey. But one of her requests was ignored. In her will she had given orders that her body should be used for dissection in a teaching hospital. It was not, and she was buried in the family vault under the epitaph "F.N. Born 1820. Died 1910".

Florence Nightingale possessed extraordinary gifts and good fortune. She was intelligent, caring and strong. She had the confidence of the upper classes and the guile to use her personal connections to manipulate those in power to fulfil her schemes.

Her determination and rare selflessness brought about radical changes in society's attitude to women, and, through the Nightingale School of Nursing, formed the basis of nursing today.

Florence Nightingale, aged 71.

Find Out More ...

Important Dates

1820	Born in Florence, Italy.
1837	Tours Europe. Queen Victoria comes to the throne.
1839	Presented at court.
1844	Begins visiting hospitals.
1849	Refuses marriage.
1851	Works at Kaiserswerth.
1853	Appointed Superintendent of the Institution for the Care of Sick Gentlewomen.
1854	Outbreak of the Crimean War. Leads nursing mission to Scutari.
1855	Catches "Crimean fever" at Balaklava.
1856	Returns to England and meets Queen Victoria.
1857	Rebellion in India. Appointment of Royal Commission on army health.
1860	Nightingale School of Nursing established. *Notes on Nursing* published.
1861–5	American Civil War.
1867	Advises on the improvement of nursing in hospitals for the poor.
1868	Helps establish East London Nursing Society.
1901	Loses sight. Queen Victoria dies.
1907	Awarded Order of Merit.
1910	Dies.

Useful Information

Florence Nightingale Museum
2 Lambeth Palace Road
London
SE1 7EW
www.florence-nightingale.co.uk

Florence Nightingale School of Nursing and Midwifery
School Support Services
King's College London
57 Waterloo Road
London
SE1 8WA

The Department of Health
Richmond House
79 Whitehall
London
SW1A 2NS
www.doh.gov.uk

The Florence Nightingale Foundation
Ground Floor, York House
199 Westminster Bridge Road
London
SE1 7UT
www.florence-nightingale-foundation.org.uk

Glossary

Dispatches Accounts of news sent from a distant place.

Epidemic A widespread outbreak of disease.

Freedom of the City of London The right to live in London without paying local taxes. In practice, a way of recognizing a person's outstanding achievements or qualities. Usually the person is presented with a handsome scroll at a banquet.

Habit A uniform worn by nuns; each order may have its own distinctive habit.

Leeches Small, slug-like water creatures which suck out blood when in contact with human or animal skin; used in traditional medicine which blamed "bad blood" for many illnesses.

Minister to Take care of.

Order An organization, often founded by a saint, which follows a particular set of rules for the worship of God and the service of others.

Order of Merit A high-ranking award established by King Edward VII (1901–10) to honour civilians outside government and the armed forces for their service to Britain.

Orderlies Junior hospital attendants.

Patriotism A strong belief in one's country.

Plenary Full.

Probationer nurses Nurses serving a period of training as an apprenticeship.

Requisite A needed item.

Royal Commission An independent, high-level committee appointed by government to look into a problem and recommend changes.

Salvation A means of saving from injury or evil.

Tsar The traditional title of Russian rulers; from the Russian word for Caesar.

Tyranny An oppressive rule with no certain rights for the ruled.

Index

Picture Acknowledgements

The publishers would like to thank the following for providing the photographs in this book: BBC Hulton Picture Library Frontispiece,4 (both),5,6 (both), 7,8,9,10 (both),11 (both),12,13,14 (both),15,16,17 (both),19,20,22,23,25,26,27, 28 (both),29,31; Mary Evans Picture Library 24; National Army Museum 18,21 (both).